Fine Dining for Babies

written and created by
Adam Crockett

with photography from
Haydon Perrior

Fine Dining for Babies
© 2024 Dokument Press
& Adam Crockett
Photography by Haydon Perrior

ISBN 978-91-88369-86-4
Printed in Poland
First edition

Dokument Press
Årstavägen 26
12052 Årsta
Sweden

hello@dokumentpress.com
dokumentpress.com
@dokumentpress

4 Introduction

8 The Dietary Dance

10 The Art of Breakfast

22 Haute Highchair Couture

24 Exquisite Entrées

34 Tasteful Tableware

36 Weaning with Meaning

48 Masterful Mains

66 The Diaper Sommelier

68 Decadent Desserts

82 A Post Dinner Lullaby

84 Acknowledgements

Baptism by Béarnaise

Ancient Rome may have invented the land of gladiatorial combat, majestic aqueducts and conquered half of Europe. But whilst all this dilly-dallying was taking place, babies across the country were chewing on stale pieces of bread and odd bits of bone for teething exercises. They made do with donkey's milk as a motherly alternative and used honey-soaked rags as makeshift dummies.

It's no wonder therefore, that with all this un-chic dining for babies, no-one born in Ancient Rome ever grew up to invent the smartphone or forge a 7-figure salary trading in blue chip companies.

But as time has developed, children's meals have become more elevated. The stale bread has been outed, and in has come more sophisticated weaning sticks – and iPhones. It's clear that when we take greater care in what we choose to feed our tots both their lives, and ours, become more prosperous. So why should the wonders of Michelin-level meals be reserved only for when we've outgrown highchairs?

It's time we introduced our offspring to the finer foods in life, earlier in life. It's time we taught them about the subtle notes of vintage purées and redefined baby food from merely adorable to avant-garde. Instead of betting our children's future on bottom-shelf baby food we need to elevate the meals we give our babies to the highest of culinary standards. So that one day, your two-year-old will be using their abacus to formulate fiscal budgets and leading global conferences from the confines of their playpen, all whilst chewing on hand-rolled pappardelle.

Within these pages lies the ultimate blueprint to baby gastronomy. Discover a world of beautiful bruncheons, exquisite entrées and posh purée recipes for those 6-36 months old.

There's no reservations required, cashmere bibs are optional and milk pairings are on the house.

Bon appétit, bébés.

The
Dietary
Dance

Before we begin to indulge in the world of highchair dining, it's important to remember that over the course of 6-36 months, the types of foods suitable for your baby will change.

Each recipe comes with a suggested age pairing but of course, each child is different. So, please adjust when and where you feel comfortable.

It's key to make sure the size of your chopped ingredients aligns with your loved one's age. It is recommended that at 6-8 months old, you prepare food that is large enough for your baby to pick up independently, as most choking occurs when food is placed straight into their mouths. This means food pieces the length and width of two adult fingers, or longer than your tot's closed fist, work well. At 9-12 months, your baby should be able to consume ruler-thin slices and small, bite size pieces. And after 12 months, you can begin to introduce utensils and let them experiment with different food sizes, keeping a keen eye on them to avoid any accidents.

When it comes to salt, it is recommended that this is not introduced before 12 months and that your baby does not exceed more than 2g per day after this. Added sugar should also be avoided before 12 months and ideally, not introduced until after 24 months.

Always consult your child's doctor before introducing any new flavours and ingredients, particularly with nuts, and begin with small doses. Watch for strong responses and if there's signs of discomfort or any allergic reaction, please contact medical help immediately.

Each recipe comes with a serving suggestion based on an 18 month old child, so please feel free to adjust serving sizes to match your baby's current diet.

And finally, please be advised that the recipes are to be followed at one's own discretion and liability.

Every morning is another opportunity to kick-start your offspring's trajectory towards world domination.

Breakfasts, or bruncheons, lay the vital energy foundations babies need to master their gurgling repertoire and leverage corporate play dates throughout their formative weeks. But it isn't just about surviving the rigours of diaper diplomacy, it's about securing their VIP place in the playground of global giants later on in life too.

The cognitive prowess of babies skyrockets when a nutritious breakfast is consumed, with increased memory and laser-focused attention. This is hugely important as they climb the educational ladder and it could be the difference between your tot becoming a standard start-up CEO and a future Fortune 500 leader.

In this section, you will learn how to master the art of marvellous morning meals, from dippy quail eggs with sour dough soldiers to flower petal muesli. So, let's raise a silver spoonful of farm-to-highchair purée and make breakfast a lucrative investment for your tiny tycoon.

Flower Petal Muesli

Introduce your tot to the wonders of the botanical world with edible flowers. Encourage your loved one to play with the petals and develop the essential flower arranging proficiencies required later in life.

Duration	The time it takes to prune the topiaries at the Palace of Versailles (40 minutes)
Serves	2 (recommended for 6+ months)
Ingredients	45 grams | 1.6 ounces rolled organic oats
	45 grams | 1.6 ounces plain yogurt
	3 tablespoons smooth Jersey milk (or breast milk)
	20 grams | 0.7 ounces strawberries
	20 grams | 0.7 ounces raspberries
	20 grams | 0.7 ounces blueberries
	a handful of edible Viola flower petals

Method

Chop the berries into quarters, creating a medley of this season's finest fruits.

Mingle the fruits with the organic oats, creamy yogurt, milk and golden honey.

Consign to the cool recesses of your double-door refrigerator for a period of 4 hours, allowing the flavours to court one another in graceful harmony.

Upon serving, garnish delicately with a gentle sprinkling of ethereal flower petals. Serve with poise, and let your child savour the elegant fusion of tastes and aromas.

Ibérico Ham Omelette

Duration	The completion of a tax return in the Cayman Islands (10 minutes)
Serves	1 - 2 (recommended for 12+ months)

Ingredients

1 large Burford Brown egg
½ tablespoon single organic cream
7 grams | ¼ ounce unsalted farm butter
20 grams | ¾ ounces Jamón Ibérico De Bellota
25 grams | 1 ounce Swiss gruyère
½ stem of chive

Method

Whisk the egg with a dollop of velvety cream in a bowl for 10 seconds, achieving a light foam.

Chop the Ibérico ham into petite morsels. Melt the butter in a pan and cook the ham until warmed then, set the ham aside.

Coax the remaining butter into a graceful swirl in the pan. Briskly whisk the eggs before decanting them into the pan. Allow a brief respite of 30 seconds or until the very periphery of your omelette sets. Then, with a light touch, stroke across the pan. Lift the cooked egg whilst letting the uncooked portion find its way to the base. Continue this elegant dance for another half minute.

Grate the gruyère atop one half, following with the previously warmed Ibérico ham.

Loosen the omelette's edge and daintily fold over. Allow it to remain in the pan for an additional 30 seconds, permitting the cheese to melt and the interior to finish its culinary metamorphosis.

Lastly, chop the chives and sprinkle over with a flourish before serving.

Dippy Quail Eggs and Sourdough Soldiers

Duration   The ascent to the peak of the Swiss Alps (18 minutes)

Serves   2 (recommended for 6+ months)

Ingredients   3 slices of sourdough bread
2 quail eggs
1 tablespoon lightly-whipped French butter
a small handful of fresh chives
a pinch of parsley

Method   Preheat your oven to 180°C | 350°F. Take two slices of sourdough and flatten them using a rolling pin. Lightly brush all sides with melted French butter and use the remainder to grease two ramekins.

Place one slice of bread into each ramekin, pressing them gently against the sides to form a basket shape. Then, fill with a cracked egg and bake in the oven for about 10-12 minutes.

Toast the remaining slice of bread and cut it into soldiers before removing the cooked ramekins from the oven and garnishing them with herbs. Leave to cool then serve.

Overnight Chia Oats

You may want to consider onboarding your toddler to help you with this recipe. The careful sequencing and layering of ingredients could likely be the moment that kick starts a prosperous career in coding.

Duration A leisurely gondola trip through Venice including moments to reflect (10 ½ hours)

Serves 1 (recommended for 6+ months)

Ingredients
1 ½ tablespoons rolled oats
½ tablespoon chia seeds
60 millilitres | ¼ cup breast or Jersey milk
1 diamond red strawberry
4 organic blueberries
1 teaspoon finely ground almonds
a sprinkle of finely ground cinnamon

Method In a crystal teddy jar, unite the chia seeds, fine oats, and mother's milk. Stir diligently until a sublime mixture is achieved and all of the chia seeds are thoroughly soaked and blended.

Deposit within the chilled confines of your double-door refrigerator and allow it to rest overnight. Should you be in a rush, a minimum repose of 3 hours may suffice.

Chop the strawberries and blueberries, using them to adorn your overnight chia seed oats and conclude with a delicate dusting of cinnamon and ground almonds.

Haute Highchair Couture

Fine dining for babies doesn't just come down to what's on the plate. It's key that your child dresses the part too.

Wearing smart attire at mealtimes helps emphasise the occasion and thus instils a sense of routine. It teaches our little angels to prepare for mealtimes in a way which is respectful of others and promotes proper cleanliness and responsibility.

So, what couture should be hanging in your child's culinary closet?

It goes without saying that pyjamas should stay reserved for bedtime tales. Instead, you'll find your baby is far more likely to boost their self-confidence when donning a three piece suit. Remember to ask your tot's tailor to use only 100% cotton materials and implement elastic waistband solutions – after all, dining can be an expansive experience and it will make diaper changes easier. Children also have much more sensitive skin than adults and they find it harder to regulate temperatures – so they need soft, breathable waistcoats. But no polyester or nylon... Let's reserve such travesties for camping tents.

When it comes to bibs, it might be tempting to veer towards cashmere – its plush allure is undeniable. But for the chic epicurean in training, nothing beats the lavish pragmatism of a 700-thread count Egyptian cotton bib.

And as your child grows a little older and begins to grow their lunch box collection, we recommend staying clear of colourful plastics and instead opt for black leather satchels reminiscent of a an attaché case. You'll find your child will not only hold their sandwiches with more gravitas but also stride with a new-found dignity.

With just a few small tweaks to your loved one's attire, you'll see the world of difference. So remember, meals start in the custom-fitted wardrobe and only culminate at the 14-seater dining table.

Even with large family trusts, things don't always happen overnight. Sometimes you have to navigate international time zones and wait for checks to clear. It can often take up to two or three days.

So, just as it's important to introduce your child to new foods and flavours in small quantities, it's equally vital that your child understand the need to take smaller, more calculated, steps at times. And what better exemplifies this than entrées? They're a culinary prelude that not only whets the appetite but also teaches the merits of patience and anticipation.

These smaller plates are essential for limiting the overwhelming feelings of yet-to-be-tried ingredients and instead offer confidence to face the big challenges ahead, whether that be a main course or a daunting teddy bear tribunal.

Never shy away from preparing something more modest now and again. It's not an admittance of failure but a stage-setting for future success.

Sweet Potato Smileys

By assigning emotions to Spanish sweet potato smileys you can increase your child's emotional intelligence, which can lead to efficient conflict resolution in the playground and soon, in the boardroom too.

Duration The deep clean of a 10-seater Gulfstream jet (2 ½ hours)

Serves 4 (recommended for 6+ months)

Ingredients 200 grams | 7 ounces cooked Natoora Yukon potato
125 grams | 4 ½ ounces cooked organic sweet potato
100 grams | 3 ½ ounces plain wholemeal flour
½ organic white egg
extra virgin olive oil

Method Set your oven to 180°C | 350°F

Marry the sweet potato and gold potatoes, mashing them to perfection. Introduce the flour with a robust beating and then add the egg, mixing until blended.

Press the mixture into a lined tray, forming an even layer 1 cm | ½ inch in thickness and allow to cool in a refrigerator until firm

Use a round cutter to sculpt circles. Then, employing a straw, fashion eyes, and with a small knife, etch mouths to bring your smileys to life.

Coat with virgin olive oil. Place in the oven and bake for 30 minutes until they achieve a golden hue and serve.

Children's Charcuterie

Duration	A comprehensive chandelier consultation (1 hour)
Serves	4 (recommended for 24+ months)
Ingredients	200 millilitres	1 cup of hummus
	1 tablespoons Icelandic skyr
	1 tablespoons extra virgin olive oil
	a sprinkle of sumac
	1 tablespoons chopped parsley

Ingredients

200 millilitres | 1 cup of hummus
1 tablespoons Icelandic skyr
1 tablespoons extra virgin olive oil
a sprinkle of sumac
1 tablespoons chopped parsley

9 heirloom carrots of various colours (dragon purple, lunar white, and solar yellow)
Castelvetrano and Picholine pitted olives
2 honeycrisp apples
10 Muscat grapes
5 artisanal grissini breadsticks
5 water biscuits
50 grams | 2 ounces Black Forest ham
50 grams | 2 ounces prosciutto
80g | 3 ounces mild Cheddar
80g | 3 ounces baby Swiss or Jarlsberg
80g | 3 ounces aged Gouda

Method   Commence by crafting your dip. You may wish to use
pre-made hummus or make your own by blending
chickpeas, tahini, lemon juice, garlic, and a bit of water
until smooth, adjusting the consistency with water as
needed.

Carefully combine the hummus and Icelandic skyr and
mix well.

In a separate bijou bowl, combine the extra virgin olive
oil, sumac, and chopped parsley. Gently mix them
together.

Decant the hummus and skyr, blend into a bespoke
serving vessel and artfully drizzle the sumac and parsley
elixir atop.

Now, cleanse and skin the carrots before chopping them
into small batons to create a rainbow of carrot sticks.

In a similar fashion, cut the cheese into delectable
slivers and segment the olives and grapes into quarters.

Conclude by sculpting the honeycrisp apple into dainty
portions.

Display with prowess on an elegant silver platter.

Curly Kale Crisps

This healthy alternative to crisps is the perfect snack to pop in a handbag for those long chauffeured journeys home following uncomfortably impressive baby ballet recitals.

Duration $1/140,160$ th of the time it took Michelangelo to complete the Sistine Chapel ceiling (15 minutes)

Serves 1 (recommended for 12+ months)

Ingredients 50 grams | 2 ounces Pentland Brig kale
a small pinch of Hungarian sweet paprika
1 ½ tablespoons extra virgin olive oil

Method Preheat the oven to 180°C | 350°F.

Rinse the fresh kale, allowing the water to cascade through the leaves, and drain. Pat dry and remove the central stalks. Tear the leaves into intricate small pieces.

Sprinkle the sweet paprika on the kale and marry with a splash of olive oil. Mix and ensure every piece of kale is coated.

Lay and curate the kale on a tray. Bake for 10 minutes, until the leaves have crisped to perfection, their colour should be softened.

Allow it to cool and serve with sophistication.

Forks *and* Fortunes

In the illustrious journey of nurturing young gourmands, the art of table setting maintains the utmost importance. It's a world where exquisite meals and equally extraordinary tableware must dance in harmony.

As the dust settles following a birth, there's often one question that's on the tip of every new mother's tongue: when can one introduce a child to the world of silver cutlery?

It's not recommended that your child has a silver spoon in their mouth from day one. But fear not, you shouldn't have to wait long. The common consensus is that 18 months is a good time for introducing shiny utensils. Begin with the spoon followed by the fork, and finally, the knife: a triumvirate of silver sophistication.

And although it may go against your deep-rooted beliefs, begin with silver-plated utensils so you can nurture young ones' delicate muscles before graduating to heftier, solid silver counterparts. Fascinatingly, should your child's attention wander during meal times later in life, it can be useful to utilise even weightier cutlery to help anchor their focus.

After mastering silverware, you'll want to tackle the crystal conundrum.

It's a little tricker to put a numeric age on when you should be introducing crystal, as glassware should really be integrated only once children have a good grasp of comprehending instructions. Embrace this special moment when it comes. There's a unique delight in watching your little one delicately manoeuvre a hand-crafted crystal egg cup and hearing them say "Swarovski" for the first time is a delightful testament to their budding affinity for life's more luxurious treasures.

From opulent utensils to glorious glassware, always aim to make sure your loved ones' place settings become as refined as their palates.

Born to Wear

A time comes for us all where we must step out of the shadow of our mother's breasts and into the limelight. A time when we transition from the comforting cradle of milk to the more cosmopolitan realms of artisanal delicacies.

Weaning, the journey of discovering solid foods, is often embarked on around the 6-month mark and it plays a pivotal role in babies' jaw development. Just as mummy and daddy may indulge in a spot of reformer pilates or equestrian yoga, each chew can be a tiny workout for our loved ones. And whilst many may see weaning as mere teething exercise, it's also a major step for babies as they cut their teeth in the corporate world too.

Weaning is children's first taste of patient self-serving. These initial forays into anticipatory gastronomic indulgence serve as the bedrock for impeccable work-dinner etiquette. After all, the last thing you would want is a son or daughter that thinks it's ok to hurriedly reach across the table at a state dinner because they hadn't properly indulged in the art of self-restraint during their weaning soirées.

So, relish this chapter in your child's journey and look forward to the treasure it will unveil knowing that one can't win at life, without first winning at weaning.

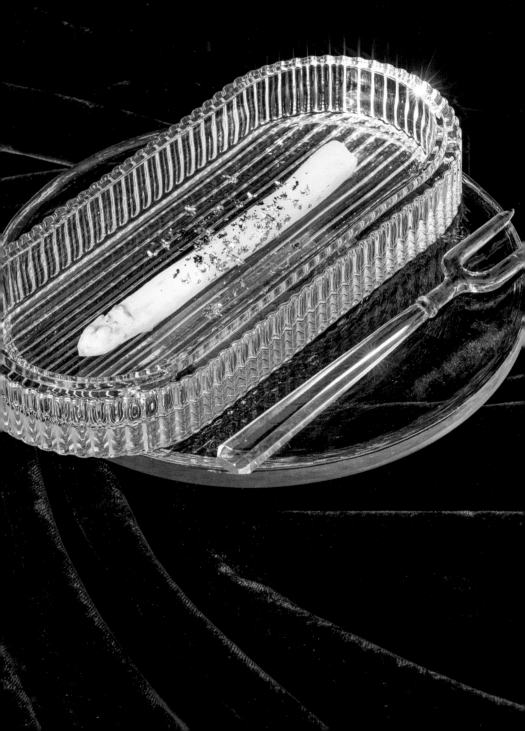

White Asparagus Weaning Stick

Thanks to the shape and size of these white asparagus weaning sticks, you can give your child an early idea of what it's like to lift a Mont Blanc. Introducing this feeling to those in their first months can be paramount to shaping young hands that will one day pen monumental deals.

Duration	The $92,000,000 bidding war on Edvard Munch's 'The Scream' (12 minutes)
Serves	1 (recommended for 6+ months)
Ingredients	2 white asparagus stems 500 millilitres | 2 cups water
Method	Delicately peel your asparagus, then slice lengthways three times and remove the thicker base. Steam the asparagus until soft, this usually takes about 10 minutes. Serve on a delicate tray. You may also wish to adorn with some gold leaf flakes.

Cinnamon Carrot Sticks

Long relegated to the depths of school lunch boxes, this elegant take on the humble carrot stick will be the crown jewels to your baby's weaning journey. A golden touch of cinnamon not only introduces sweeter flavours without a speck of sugar, but flaunts remarkable natural anti-inflammatory properties too.

Duration The average commute in Luxembourg (29 minutes)

Serves 1 (recommended for 6+ months)

Ingredients 5 organic baby carrots
½ tablespoon Tuscan olive oil
a sprinkle of ground cinnamon

Method Preheat the oven to 200°C | 400°F.

In a bowl, cut carrots into 2-3 inch sticks and coat evenly with olive oil. Follow with a sprinkle of cinnamon.

Ready a baking tray, dressing it with parchment paper, and artfully arrange the carrot batons, ensuring they luxuriate in their own space.

Bake for 18-20 minutes, allowing them to reach a temperature at which a steel knife can tenderly melt through the body of the carrot.

Allow them to cool and present with a touch of elegance.

Buffalo Mozzarella Cheese Strings

Duration The re-calibration of a Rolex Datejust (20 minutes)

Serves 1 (recommended for 6+ months)

Ingredients 40 grams | 1.4 ounces Neapolitan mozzarella di bufala
1 ½ litres | 2 pints water

Method Gently shred the mozzarella into pieces the size of a white gold watch's clock face.

Pour your water into a polished stainless steel pot, bringing it to a hot, yet not steaming, temperature. Tenderly add the shredded cheese, and allow it to repose for 2 minutes.

Carefully remove 2 tablespoons of the melted mozzarella at a time. Stretch until it becomes firm and gleams with a glossy finish.

Roll and fold the cheese to shape elegant sticks.

Allow the sticks to cool, awaiting the moment when they can be peeled away like a mozzarella umbrella.

Plating Up Prosperity

Main courses are the pillar to every great meal. As anticipation builds up with the consumption of entrées, these central dishes bear the heavy weight of expectations.

But these lavish plates aren't just the focal point for luncheons and suppers; they're developmental milestones that teach your child about seizing life's big moments. Because once the table is cleared and fresh cutlery is placed, and as all eyes eagerly scan for the first glimpse of the platter and silver sippy-cups are raised, it's time to stand up and be counted. It's in these pivotal junctures where your child will learn that hesitation rarely garners acclaim.

Gathering around to enjoy the main course isn't just an opportunity for your child either, it's a golden opportunity for parents too. For it's not just the food that you pass onto your offspring, but the accumulated wisdom of your years. Dinners can become profound trading strategy discussions, imparting insights into commerce's finer nuances. Luncheons can be a time to impart the tales of your property portfolio and share the time-tested secrets of thoroughbred horse racing that have been handed down from generation to generation.

So recline into the depths of your mahogany chair, and enjoy the pièce de résistance.

Bilingual Alphabet Soup

Looking to get your child's French polished ahead of Monaco? Let mealtimes be a moment for learning secondary languages with this homemade bilingual alphabet soup recipe.

Duration   The average F1 race (1 ½ hours)

Serves   3 - 4 (recommended for 6+ months)

Ingredients   2 large organic brown eggs
185 grams | 6 ½ ounces Italian Tipo "00" Flour

1 ½ teaspoons Tuscan olive oil
½ sliced Duchy organic carrot
¼ diced rose Roscoff onion
1 clove organic white garlic
100 grams | 3 ½ ounces Italian tomato passata
100 millilitres | ½ cup homemade chicken broth
120 grams | 4 ounces Pome Dei Moro tomatoes
ground Wayanad peppercorns

Method *To make the pasta:*

Create a small pyramid with your fine Italian flour and using the tips of your fingers, scoop a well. Crack your eggs into the well and whisk with a fork. Mix the smooth eggs into the flour. Take your time – Boléro can provide the soundtrack to keep you at the right pace.

Begin to knead the dough until it feels silky and then let it rest in your refrigerator for 40 minutes.

After dusting your kitchen island's soapstone counter, roll out the dough to a thickness of 2-3 mm | 0.1 inch.

Carefully use small alphabet cutters from your chosen languages, whether that is indeed French or even Chinese, and place the pasta letters to the side.

To make the soup:

Heat a small pot over medium heat, add Tuscan olive oil and sauté the carrots, onion and garlic until they begin to soften.

Peel the Pome Dei Moro tomatoes and then chop into quarters.

Add the passata and chopped tomatoes and bring to a boil before adding the chicken broth. Season with your pepper then turn down to a simmer for 12-14 minutes. You can add additional water if needed.

Add your bilingual alphabet pasta pieces and cook for 1-5 minutes depending on thickness.

Once cooked through, it's time to say "Bon appétit".

Tarragon Turkey Dinosaurs

If there's one thing you can guarantee for your child's first few weeks at school, it's that they'll inevitably learn about dinosaurs. So give your toddler a head start on their fellow pupils by introducing these ancient beasts over dinner.

Educational highlights might encompass the disparity in wingspan between the Quetzalcoatlus and the Hatzegopteryx or consider how regions densely inhabited by dinosaurs can provide crucial insights into potential oil field locations.

It's also worth noting, that if you're struggling to introduce your little loved one to new foods and flavours, employing creative shapes and storytelling can make it effortless.

Duration   A Chanel ready-to-wear show (15 minutes)

Serves   2 (recommended for 6+ months)

Ingredients   100 grams | 3 ½ ounces organic turkey thigh mince
3 spears of asparagus
2 tablespoons sourdough breadcrumbs
½ clove organic white garlic
1 teaspoon freshly chopped tarragon leaves
1 organic brown egg
ground Wayanad peppercorns
Sicilian olive oil
organic green leaves

Method   Preheat your oven to 180°C | 350°F.

Combine the turkey mince, white garlic and tarragon leaves and mix well in a bowl. Season with pepper.

With a separate container, beat the egg with assured composure before adding your turkey mince mix, making sure everything is thoroughly amalgamated.

Pick up a small handful of the mixture and, with a rolling pin, roll it into small sheets. You can then use your hands to shape the sheets into dinosaurs, or if you'd rather, use a dinosaur-shaped cutter.

Once all the mixture has been formed into tyrannosauruses and teradactyls, coat the sides with sourdough breadcrumbs. Make sure each side is evenly coated.

Place on a preheated skillet and cook for 4-5 minutes on each side, or until golden and cooked through.

Season the asparagus with a dash of olive oil and pepper before steaming for 3-4 minutes or until soft.

Serve the dinosaurs on top of the bed of asparagus and green leaves on a fine porcelain platter.

Gold Leaf PB&J

Duration	The dressage judging time limit (10 minutes)
Serves	1 (recommended for 24+ months)
Ingredients	2 slices of farmhouse white bread
	50 grams | 1.8 ounces organic strawberries
	1 tablespoon no-added sugar peanut butter
	½ teaspoon golden acacia runny honey
	½ teaspoon edible pure gold leaf flakes
Method	Begin by chopping the strawberries into eighths, transforming them into dainty portions.

Heat a Le Creuset pan to a medium embrace and add the honey, followed by the strawberry pieces.

Once simmering, press down on the strawberries with a spoon, melding them into a sweet mash. Stirring for approximately 5 minutes, before decanting into a waiting bowl.

As you await the strawberry mix to achieve room temperature, generously coat your bread slices with peanut butter.

Next, spread your homemade strawberry jam and sprinkle it with gold leaf flakes.

Finally, cut the sandwich into perfect triangles and serve.

Truffle
Pizzettes

Duration   A yacht christening (2 ½ hours)

Serves   2 (recommended for 6+ months)

Ingredients   75 grams | 2 ½ ounces Italian Tipo "00" Flour
65 millilitres | ¼ cup warm water
⅓ teaspoon fast-acting yeast
6 baby chestnut mushrooms
½ purple garlic clove
1 teaspoon extra virgin olive oil
70 grams | 2 ½ ounces of Italian buffalo mozzarella
a small handful of Parmigiano Reggiano
a splash of white truffle oil
marinara tomato sauce
wild rocket

Method   To compose the pizza dough, place the flour, yeast and water into a bowl and mix well. Cover with a tea towel of the finest Irish linen and rest for a couple of hours.

Meanwhile, chop the mushrooms into consumable pieces and mince the garlic.

When the dough announces its readiness, heat the oven to 200°C | 400°F, or employ the heat of a wood-fire pizza oven if available.

Place the dough upon a flour-dusted pizza plate, stretching it into a perfect circle, 1cm | ½ inch in thickness – a canvas in waiting. You may wish to add the tomato sauce at this stage.

Brush with olive oil, and grate the cheeses atop before adding the mushrooms and minced garlic. Cook until the mozzarella and Parmigiano Reggiano have melted. This should take around 6 minutes in a conventional oven.

Finish with a splash of truffle oil and some rocket then allow to cool and serve.

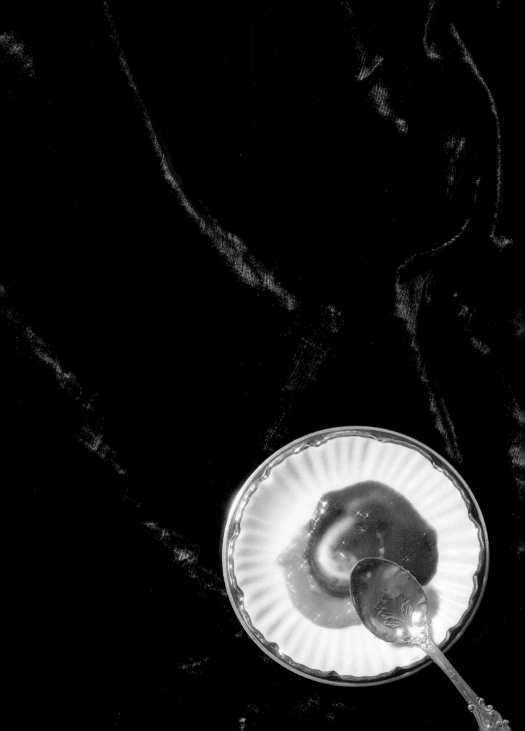

Puréed Amuse-Bouche

Turning one. Stepping into a classroom for the first time. That moment you spot a shiny new hobbyhorse.

Memories from our younger years may be few and far between, but one thing we never forget, is our first amuse-bouche. So, relish this rite of passage with the following recipe by crafting three sumptuous purées for your tiny tot: a medley of beetroot and plum, the pairing of tenderstem broccoli with a hint of basil, and a ravishing blend of aubergine and sweet potato.

Duration A polo match, excluding halftime divot stomping (1 hour)

Serves 2 (recommended for 6+ months)

Ingredients 2 sun-kissed plums
1 small beetroot

2 small heads of tenderstem broccoli
1 modest bouquet of organic Genovese basil leaves

1 small Japanese sweet potato
1 small aubergine

Method Peel the beetroot and sweet potato then remove the pits from the plums. Chop all the ingredients into small, even-sized cubes and make sure to remove any seeds from the aubergine.

Steam the sweet potato and aubergine pieces for 10-15 minutes, until soft.

Separately, steam the beetroot with for 15-20 minutes. Insert a silver fork and make sure it can easily go through the beetroot.

Separately, steam the broccoli until it becomes tender. This should take about 5-7 minutes.

Then, bring a small pot of water to a boil and prepare a side bowl of ice. Quickly blanch the basil leaves by dipping them into the boiling water for just a few seconds, then immediately transfer them to the ice water and drain.

Using a blender, mix the aubergine and sweet potato together, followed independently by the blending of the beetroot and plum. And finally, blend the tenderstem broccoli and basil to create three separate purées. If the consistency is too thick, you can add a little breast milk or formula to thin it out as desired.

With an artistic touch, use a small spoon to create gentle swirls with the purees on a platter and serve.

Monkfish Fingers

Duration	A champagne sabrage class (40 minutes)
Serves	2 (recommended for 6+ months)
Ingredients	1 medium monkfish tail
	3 slices of stonebaked bread
	1 organic brown egg
	200 grams | 7 ounces organic plain flour
	2 tablespoons fresh Italian rosemary
	100 grams | 3 ½ ounces Parmigiano Reggiano
	¼ tablespoon black pepper
	A splash of cold-pressed rapeseed oil
	A handful of watercress
	A handful of organic rocket
	A teaspoon unsalted butter
	100 grams | 3 ½ ounces petit pois
Method	Carefully debone the monkfish.

With a touch of rustic charm, blend the artisanal bread slices to create crumbs.

Grate the Parmigiano Reggiano and break apart the rosemary into pieces. Unite with the breadcrumbs.

Crack the egg into a bowl, and whisk.

Cut the monkfish into finger-sized strips. Then, dip one of the strips into the egg wash, followed by the flour, and finally the breadcrumb mixture. Repeat this for each strip and place in the refrigerator for 5-15 minutes.

Heat a pan until the oil begins to dance and introduce the fingers to its warm bath. Cook until golden, or until the monkfish is fully cooked through.

Meanwhile, place the petit pois in a large skillet with the butter and sauté on medium heat until cooked.

Craft a bed of watercress, rocket and petit pois, and carefully lay your golden monkfish fingers atop. You may desire to serve with an additional sprinkling of rosemary.

The
Diaper
Sommelier

They say you're never long out of the frying pan before you're into the fire. And indeed, such wisdom holds true.

Whether you call them diapers, or nappies, we all know that these precious padded protectors hold a gastronomic history of our young one's recent repast. But were you aware that you can deduce what your infant has eaten with just a whiff? See, not only can you become an expert in cooking baby food but identifying it afterwards too.

You may be wondering why this skill would be useful. Well, on the off chance that you're not personally curating your offspring's meals, this ability ensures you can check that they're still partaking in the crème de la crème of infant nourishment. Now you can be privy to any sneaky sub-par biscuits during a playdate and quickly discern if the nursery's offerings truly justify its princely invoice.

So, what aromas should you be looking out for?

Well, if you're finding strong metallic top notes it's likely that this is due to your child consuming asparagus. A moment to cherish. 'Briny' scents are another exciting discovery. These are produced after seafood such as salmon and monkfish. You'll also want to get some methane and sulphurous base notes, which signify a diet rich in proteins and vegetables respectively. And fear not if your child is producing unscented symphonies. This could mean that they've been eating lots of probiotics, fruits like apples, pears, and bananas and whole grains. All of which are glorious for your baby's gut flora.

However, on a rare occasion, you may come across digestion deposits that smell unusually chemical and sickly sweet. These are the signifiers that your child has unfortunately come across over-processed foods. In case of this, try to keep yourself composed and embark on a little detective work to trace the origin. Only once you have found the potential source, should you call your friend, who's a lawyer, to discuss next steps.

Practice makes perfect, so use every diaper change as an opportunity to refine your nose because safeguarding gourmet standards starts from the bottom up.

The Sweet Taste of Success

No-one wants to raise just another player in the sandbox of life, we want our offspring to be the architect of boardroom decisions. We want them sitting firmly in the skies of high-rise financial districts, comfortably perched in the finest of silk suits, and a crucial ingredient to attaining this is great desserts.

See, desserts are not merely about appeasing tiny taste buds or marking the end of a meal. They're about teaching toddlers an early appreciation for the rewards that follow hard work. They're the treat at the end of a long day deciphering lullabies. They're the sweet compensation to the occasional drool-filled drama that makes it all worthwhile.

In this chapter, you'll become proficient in crafting captivating confections, from the succulent tastes of a Madagascan Milkshake to the velvety caress of Bora Bora Baked Alaska.

Bora Bora Baked Alaska

Jet-setting isn't quite the champagne and caviar affair it used to be before children came along, so heading to the sand-drenched beaches of Bora Bora on a bi-monthly basis, may no longer be quite as attractive a prospect as it once was. But nevertheless, you can still acquaint your child with the sweet taste of French Polynesia thanks to this baked alaska, infused with fruits found in Bora Bora.

What it lacks in views of crystalline waters, it makes up for in fewer paparazzi disturbances.

Duration   The tuning of a Steinway grand piano (1 ½ hours)

Serves   4 (recommended for 24+ months)

Ingredients   50 grams | 1.8 ounces French whipped butter
50 grams | 1.8 ounces caster Sugar
1 brown egg
40 grams | 1 ½ ounces Italian 00 flour
1 tablespoon fresh milk

2 large free-range egg whites
75 grams | 2 ½ ounces caster sugar
50 grams | 1.8 ounces papaya
50 grams | 1.8 ounces mango
250 millilitres | 1 cup vanilla bean gelato

Method   Preheat your oven to 180°C | 350°F then, anoint a small round cake tin with butter and line with parchment paper.

In a ceramic bowl, add the French butter and sugar then whisk until fluffy. Add the egg and continue to whisk. Gradually fold in the sifted flour and fresh milk.

Pour the mixture into a cake tin and bake for 15-20 minutes. Then, leave to cool.

Turn the oven to 200°C | 390°F then make the topping by whisking the egg whites until stiff. Add the sugar gently until a statuesque meringue emerges.

Chop the mango and passion fruit into delicate, small pieces.

Arrange your cooled cake base upon an opulent baking tray. With a skewer, artfully prick the cake to create a constellation of small apertures, before lavishing it with ⅔ of the fruit. Gracefully crown the fruit with your ice cream, sculpting it to form the foundation of a dome, then add the remaining fruit.

Coat with the meringue using a spatula, fashioning spikes and flares as you do so. Bake for a few precious minutes until it attains a light golden hue and serve.

Madagascan Milkshake

Duration   The time it takes for a maître d' to explain the tasting menu at a Michelin-starred restaurant (10 minutes)

Serves   2 (recommended for 6+ months)

Ingredients   350 millilitres | 1 ½ cups chilled breast milk
1 teaspoon pure Madagascar vanilla extract
a sprinkle of Madagascar vanilla bean powder
pure whipped coconut cream, optional

Method   Pour the chilled breast milk into a, preferably crystal, bottle and add the Madagascar vanilla extract.

You may wish to add swirling whipped coconut cream atop the breast milkshake.

Then, as a final touch, sprinkle just a hint of genuine Madagascar vanilla bean powder.

Serve with a soft shake.

Summer Fruits Terrine

Duration	2 truffle hunting tours (12 hours)
Serves	4 (recommended for 24+ months)
Ingredients	2 Spanish oranges
	1 red ruby grapefruit
	1 package of gelatin
	30 grams | 1 ounce raw Demerara Sugar
	a squeeze of fresh yuzu juice
	¼ teaspoon Madagascan bourbon vanilla extract

Method

Peel the fruits and slice them into suitable sizes before placing into a bowl. As you engage in this task, gently squeeze each piece to release the delectable juices.

Decant the majority of the juice into a pan, joining it with the sugar and a squeeze of yuzu. Place upon a gentle heat, letting the warmth coax the flavours harmoniously.

With the remainder of the juice, soften the gelatine for a minute or two. Unite it in the pan and elevate the heat until it commences a gentle boil, making sure the sugar and gelatine are fully dissolved.

Allow this mixture to reach room temperature and decoratively place the fruit into one of your, no-doubt many, terrine dishes. Then, pour over your juice mix.

Bestow the terrine unto the refrigerator's soothing chill, preferably throughout the night.

Upon setting to a perfect consistency, turn the terrine out and serve in all its naked splendour.

Baby
Biscotti

Duration   A direct flight from JFK to Dubai (12 hours)

Serves   4 (recommended for 24+ months)

Ingredients   75 grams | 2.6 ounces organic farm plain flour
¼ teaspoon artisanal baking powder
¼ teaspoon freshly ground Ceylon cinnamon
45 grams | 1.6 ounces muscovado sugar
½ small ripe banana
1 medium free-range, organic egg yolk
1 tablespoon avocado oil
¼ teaspoon pure Madagascar vanilla extract
25 grams | 1 ounces dried cranberries

Method   Preheat your oven to 180°C | 350°F.

Chop the dried cranberries into delicate quarters, revealing their vibrant core.

In a ceramic mixing bowl, whisk together the flour, baking powder and Muscovado sugar along with a whisper of freshly ground Ceylon cinnamon.

Gently mash the bananas, combining them with the egg and avocado oil. Add the pure Madagascar vanilla extract, and whisk with conviction until a smooth, enchanting batter forms.

Divide this mixture and pour each half onto parchment-lined baking trays. Shape the batter into slender rectangles, no thicker than a finger, and sprinkle the cranberries atop.

Bake for 22 minutes or until they stand firm with poise.

Allow to cool, then chop the loaves into refined slices. Return these pieces of biscotti to the oven's warmth for five minutes, then turn and bake for another 5 minutes until golden.

Finally, let them cool once again and serve.

Elderflower Cordial Jelly

Duration	The French Riviera's Grande Corniche drive (1 hour)
Serves	6 - 8 (recommended for 6+ months)
Ingredients	1 teaspoon cold-pressed avocado oil
	8 leaves of fine leaf gelatine
	500 millilitres | 2 cups natural spring water
	140 millilitres | ½ cup handmade elderflower cordial
	2 organic raspberries
	2 organic blackberries
	2 organic blueberries
Method	Submerge the fine leaf gelatine in chilled spring water for five minutes until they take on a softened demeanour.

Usher half of the remaining water to a gentle boil and add the gelatine leaves into the pan. Whisk until mixed.

Add the remaining water along with the elderflower cordial, stirring gently. Then, add the fruit.

Prepare your heirloom jelly mould with a brush of oil.

Pour the gelatinous mix into the mould, then retire it to the refrigerator to repose overnight.

Once solidified, turn the moulds onto a serving plate.

You may also wish to cut some of your summer berries into quarters and adorn the jelly before serving.

Twinkle, Twinkle, Little Caviar

Twinkle, twinkle, little caviar,
Born to shine, destined to go far.
You're the big fish, they're the small fry,
So look down on them like the sky.

Twinkle, twinkle, little caviar,
When it comes to merit, you've set the bar.
While some can barely crawl or walk,
You can do both, and also talk.

Twinkle, twinkle, little caviar,
You are going to go so far.

A supergroup of humans came together to make this essential culinary guide come to life.

Firstly, a massive thank you to Björn and everyone at Dokument Press for your guidance and trust.

Thank you Beatrice Ferrante for your incredible food styling, Victoria Twyman for your set design wizardry and Chris Turner for lighting everything up.

Thank you to Haydon Perrior for believing in all my slightly unhinged ideas. You're a ridiculously talented man.

Thank you to Ben and Liz Barry for all your help, your generosity never fails to amaze me.

Thank you to Rachel, for keeping me grounded as a child and never making me feel worthy of bone china plates.

Thank you to mum and dad, this book is really dedicated to you but I thought it was funnier giving it to the nannies.

And finally, thank you to Charlotte. Love ya.

Written and created by Adam Crockett
Photography by Haydon Perrior
Food styling by Beatrice Ferrante
Set design by Victoria Twyman
Photography assistance by Chris Turner
All under the watchful eye of Charlotte Barry